# GUIDELINES FOR
# ALL KINDS OF MINDS

### A Manual for Adults to Use in Their Work with Children

## Dr. Mel Levine

Educators Publishing Service, Inc.

Cambridge and Toronto

Melvin D. Levine, MD, FAAP, is Director of The Clinical
Center for the Study of Development and Learning (a
University Affiliated Program) at the University of North
Carolina. He is Professor of Pediatrics at the University of
North Carolina School of Medicine, Chapel Hill, North
Carolina.

Printed in U.S.A.

ISBN 0-8388-2098-0

Educators Publishing Service, Inc.,
75 Moulton St., Cambridge, MA 02138-1104

# Contents

# Introduction

## About *All Kinds of Minds*

*All Kinds of Minds*, a blend of fiction and nonfiction illustrating the developmental differences that exist among children, is intended to be both informative and entertaining material for elementary-school students.

Its principal characters are five children who live in the same neighborhood and who are in the same classroom in school. Each of these children has a different kind of mind that causes problems and stress in school or at home. The children's difficulties include an attention deficit, a reading disorder, memory problems, a language disorder, social skills problems, and motor problems.

During the course of the first seven chapters, related fictional anecdotes, each child comes to understand his or her mind's strengths and weaknesses. All the children learn about getting support from others, helping themselves, and building on their strengths.

The eighth and final chapter, a nonfiction review, covers important concepts and facts that appear in the preceding chapters. It also offers children additional suggestions for overcoming the effects of their learning disorders.

## The Book on Tape

The complete text, read verbatim by the author, is available on cassette tapes for students who wish to listen as they read or listen instead of read.

### Broader Applications

While *All Kinds of Minds* is directed especially toward children who are experiencing difficulties with learning and school adjustment, it is also likely that all students can benefit from its contents, which should increase their tolerance of individual differences and provide insight into their own strengths and weaknesses.

### Discussing the Contents

Unquestionably, *All Kinds of Minds* will be most meaningful if its readers and listeners have opportunities to discuss the book's contents with each other and, more importantly, with an adult who has read the book. These guidelines have been formulated to assist such an adult in helping a child or a group of children understand the personal implications of *All Kinds of Minds*.

## THE BOOK'S PURPOSES

*All Kinds of Minds* strives to attain a wide range of goals. Among the purposes of the book are the following:

1. To give children a clearer understanding of some of the common learning disorders: attention deficits, reading disorders, memory problems, language disorders, social skills problems, and motor skills problems.
2. To enable children with learning disorders to gain greater insight into the difficulties they experience in school.
3. To help children with learning disorders recognize that many other students face the same kinds of problems they confront.
4. To help children with learning disorders understand that there are good ways and poor ways to handle the stresses that they feel.
5. To assist children with learning disorders to deal with any shame and guilt they may harbor regarding their learning (and perhaps behavioral and/or social) difficulties.
6. To instill a sense of optimism—and thereby bolster or sus-

tain motivation—in children who are struggling yet doing poorly in school.

7. To explain general remedial approaches and strategies that can help children with learning problems succeed in school.

8. To demonstrate to students with learning disorders that the adults in their lives can assist them in overcoming their problems.

9. To introduce students to some of the kinds of professionals in school and in the community who can be helpful to them.

10. To stimulate students to think about and devise ways through which they can help themselves to improve their learning and productivity in school.

11. To provide a beginning vocabulary about learning disorders so that children can communicate their concerns more effectively and with greater candor.

12. To show students that learning more about their learning disorders can be entertaining and interesting so that they will be motivated to continue to acquire knowledge about learning and learning disorders.

13. To help elevate the self-esteem of children who feel unsuccessful.

14. To enable children with learning disorders to recognize that they all have strengths and that they can use these strengths to be successful and happy in school and beyond school.

15. To show students that there are "all kinds of minds" and that no one has a perfect mind.

16. To encourage *all* children to be more tolerant of learning and behavioral differences among their peers and siblings.

## THE BOOK'S ORGANIZATION

### Chapter 1

The first chapter of *All Kinds of Minds* serves as an introduction. During its first several pages, the book introduces its main characters and strongly hints that all these children experience difficulty in school. Their behaviors on the bus suggest something about the nature of their problems or their feelings about school.

The remainder of the first chapter introduces three important concepts that are further developed throughout the book: 1) the human mind, 2) the kinds of mind work, and 3) learning disorders. Chapter 1 concludes with an overview of the entire book.

### Chapters 2–7

Each of the next five chapters features a child with a common specific pattern of learning disorder. In Chapter 7, all the children in the book come together and openly discuss their strengths and weaknesses. Then they talk about their futures and how they can make use of their strengths to succeed and experience happiness in life. They also discuss what they would do if they could design the ideal school for every kind of mind.

### Chapter 8

The final chapter of *All Kinds of Minds* reviews the content presented in earlier chapters. This nonfiction portion of the book discusses in more detail each of the kinds of learning disorders illustrated by children in the preceding chapters. It delineates the specific traits or weaknesses associated with problematic attention, reading skill, memory, language ability, social skill, and motor functions. In addition, Chapter 8 provides examples of what can be done to help children who endure these disorders. A series of charts and diagrams illustrate many of the important concepts for children to understand.

## USING *ALL KINDS OF MINDS*

### Reading and/or Listening

Some children whose reading skills are not commensurate with the demands of the book can benefit from simply listening to *All Kinds of Minds* on available cassette tapes. Others whose reading skills may be somewhat better should read along with the cassette tapes. Still others will feel comfortable reading the entire book without hearing the text at the same time.

## Using All or Part of the Book

The organization of *All Kinds of Minds* makes it possible for a child to read or listen to the entire book or, alternatively, only to those parts that pertain specifically to him or her. While many children will want to go through the entire book to follow its continuing story line, such a thorough reading is not essential. The chapters about specific students (Chapters 2–6) are relatively self-contained and can be read as individual units.

## Chapter 8

Chapter 8 includes individual sections and diagrams dealing with specific disorders. These sections may be discussed in conjunction with the relevant chapters; or, alternatively, Chapter 8 can be read in its entirety as a review of important concepts and as a stimulus for further discussion.

## The Tables in These Guidelines

Pages 50–53 of these guidelines contain tables that depict differences that exist among the children in the book and other issues that transcend individual chapters.

These tables may be drawn on a chalkboard or worksheet for the children, or the children themselves may collaborate with the discussion leader to create such tables.

## The Need for Discussion

So often children with learning disorders are deprived of opportunities to discuss their underlying concerns about themselves. Moreover, they are frequently reluctant to admit that they have difficulty in school.

*All Kinds of Minds* can serve as a stimulus for open and non-threatening discussion. Such discussion is facilitated when a child receives help from an adult while reading or listening to the book.

A student is most likely to benefit from the experience when discussion takes place following each chapter. Children should be encouraged, for example, to talk about their impressions of the material. They can discuss each of the children by summarizing the nature of each child's difficulty and, when doing so, by trying to use vocabulary newly acquired from the book. The latter is especially important, since it is abundantly clear that *a child can be in much greater control of a problem if she or he has the words to describe the problem!*

Once a child has finished the entire book, it is especially important that there be some general discussion about the book's themes and about the ways in which the child's own perceptions of himself or herself have changed as a result of reading *All Kinds of Minds.*

## Some Possible Settings

The reading and concurrent discussion of *All Kinds of Minds* can take place within a wide range of settings and formats:

1. **As part of a small group learning experience.** In such an instance, the book could be read by students receiving group counseling and/or remedial academic support.
2. **As part of a class in which all children read the book.** In this case, each chapter can serve as a focal point within an elementary-school unit on learning disorders or developmental differences.
3. **As part of a class in which one child reads the book to prepare a book report.** This may be a child who is experiencing some learning problems or a child who has a friend or a sibling with such difficulties.
4. **As part of tutorial sessions.** A tutor may "assign" this book or the tapes to a student; and, during tutorial sessions, there can be some discussion of its contents and their relevance to that particular student.
5. **As part of counseling or therapy.** The reading of this book can be a shared experience between a therapist and a child; together they can discuss its contents and personal implications.
6. **As part of an attempt on the part of parents to help a child with learning difficulties.** A child and her mother and/or fa-

ther can read the book together and have informal discussions about what can be learned from the children in the book. In some instances, it might be beneficial to include siblings in this joint reading experience.

## CONTENT OF THE GUIDELINES

The following sections of these guidelines will review the individual chapters within *All Kinds of Minds* and suggest some points for discussion, some questions for students, and some activities, all of which are likely to be fruitful in any of the previously-listed settings.

# Chapter 1
# All Kinds of Minds

## STARTING THE DISCUSSION OF CHAPTER 1

Discussion can begin with some questions regarding the first day of school:

<table>
<tr><td>Questions for Children</td><td>

1. How do children feel as they head towards the school building? (Children can discuss their anxieties and/or excitement.)
2. How might a student feel when he or she has had some problems in school in the past? (Does this make someone feel very nervous or afraid at the beginning of a new school year?)

</td></tr>
</table>

## IMPORTANT CONCEPTS

### Learning Disorders

Children should be introduced to the notion that some students have weaknesses that make it hard for them to learn or to do certain kinds of things in school. These weaknesses are what we mean by *learning disorders*.

> **Points to Emphasize:**
>
> ▶ Children with learning disorders are often born with their learning disorders. It's not their fault that they have learning disorders.
> ▶ Children with learning disorders are smart; often they may feel dumb or stupid, but they're not!

*Points to Emphasize, continued*

▶ Children with learning disorders have many strengths. They are not just a bundle of weaknesses.

▶ Children with learning disorders can do well with some kinds of mind work, but they have trouble with other kinds of mind work.

▶ Often children with learning disorders don't understand their learning disorders—they don't know much about their own kinds of minds, and that's why *All Kinds of Minds* can be a big help to them.

**The Mind**

There should be some discussion about the fact that the thinking part of our brains is the mind.

**Mind Work**

The concept of "mind work" should be discussed with students. They should understand that the mind needs to perform a variety of activities or jobs. These include:

1. Staying "tuned in" or paying attention to what's important.
2. Remembering.
3. Figuring out what other people are saying and how we should say our own ideas.
4. Getting our muscles to do what we want or need them to do— for things like playing sports or writing.
5. Helping us to make and keep friends.
6. Reminding us how to behave correctly.

Functions of the mind or kinds of mind work are summarized in the chart on pages 10 and 11 of the student's book. The contents of this list should be discussed with the children.

**Activities for Children**

It might be a good idea for children to contribute to a larger list of kinds of mind work which might include such pursuits as making believe, getting organized, helping people, etc. Each child might be encouraged to draw a poster, make a collage, write a paragraph, or create a video about different kinds of mind work.

**Core Messages in Chapter 1**

1. No one has a perfect mind. (In this context, it can be helpful for an adult discussion leader to "confess" his or her current weaknesses or those that existed during childhood. The message is that it is "normal" not to be good at everything.)

2. There are many different kinds of minds; different minds possess different strengths and weaknesses and are, therefore, capable of doing different kinds of mind work well.

3. No child should feel bad about his or her kind of mind and the way it works. (Here one can introduce the idea—to be elaborated upon later—that the world needs many kinds of minds.)

# Chapter 2
# Eddie's Kind of Mind

## EDDIE AS A PERSON

Eddie, who plays a central role throughout *All Kinds of Minds*, assumes the leading role in Chapter 2. He is at once lovable and exasperating; his antics provide amusement and recurrent thematic material throughout the book.

A delightful boy, Eddie nonetheless frequently gets into trouble because he has great difficulty controlling much of his behavior. He is creative but, in so many respects, not very productive.

At the same time, Eddie is a very important role model for struggling students because he demonstrates that it is possible to be a really likable and wonderful person and yet have problems. He shows that someone can do a lot of "bad things" without being a "bad person." Eddie is also important because he exemplifies a willingness to acknowledge and work on one's problems. His candor, his willingness to understand himself, and his encouragement of others to do the same represent notable strengths on his part.

## DISCUSSING EDDIE

### Attention Deficits

Eddie typifies the child who has attention deficits that affect *both* behavior *and* learning. He exhibits the following traits that are commonly encountered among such children:

1. **Overactivity**—as seen in Eddie's need to keep going to the boy's room and his trouble sitting still in class (page 17).

4

2. **Impulsivity**—as evident in his doing many things too quickly without thinking or planning, such as his detonating the mustard container at the mall (page 32) or his tendency to write without first thinking about what he wants to say and how to say it (page 23).
3. **Trouble Concentrating**—as seen in Eddie's problems listening in school (p.18).
4. **Distractibility**—as exemplified in Eddie's tendency to listen to extraneous noises or stare out the window in class (pages 18 and 19).
5. **Free Flight of Ideas**—as manifested in Eddie's daydreams about the frog-legged submarine (page 19).
6. **Insatiability**—as exhibited in Eddie's wanting things all the time (pages 25 and 26).
7. **Poor Self-monitoring**—as revealed in Eddie's reluctance to check over his writing and math work (pages 23 and 24).

---

**Points to Emphasize:**

▶ Everybody, all children and even grownups, has trouble with attention *some* of the time. We all have moments when we just can't concentrate on what we're doing or times when we daydream or do things too quickly without thinking first.

▶ It's just that Eddie has too much trouble too often with his attention.

▶ Not all kids with attention deficits are exactly like Eddie. Some children have a lot of trouble concentrating *but do not have any behavior problems.* Others have trouble concentrating *but are not overactive.* In fact, some are kind of underactive! But they all have trouble with concentration.

---

After discussing Eddie's traits, it can be useful to have students turn to the chart on page 236 to consider how attention is supposed to work in everyone—when it's working well.

### Concentration and Impulse Control

Probably the two most important of Eddie's traits requiring further discussion and elaboration are his weak concentration and his problem with impulsivity.

---

**Points to Emphasize:**

▶ Concentration involves the ability to remain focused on the right information or the right pursuit for the right amount of time.

▶ It further entails thinking about what's most salient or important at the moment rather than being distracted or focusing upon irrelevant details.

▶ Concentration also involves being able to focus *long enough*. This means you are able to remain "tuned in" long enough to complete work or to listen to all of the directions that the teacher is communicating.

▶ There can be some discussion about how a person feels when she or he is having trouble concentrating. Most commonly, students having difficulty with attention report that they feel bored or extremely tired when they can't focus. Such a discussion may help children understand better these feelings when and if they occur in school.

▶ It can also be constructive to talk about how hard it is to get work done when you're having trouble concentrating. The example of getting homework done might be used in this context.

▶ Children should be helped to realize that if you are impulsive when you do your work, you are apt to make a lot of careless mistakes.

▶ Kids need to understand that if they act impulsively, or if they say things impulsively, they can get into trouble without meaning to at all.

---

## Thinking More about Eddie's Behavior

Eddie's behavior at home and in school raises a very important issue. Many of his actions might be referred to as "bad." In fact, much of his behavior is truly disruptive and problematic for his teacher, for other students, and for his family. The question then arises: *Is Eddie bad?*

---

**Points to Emphasize:**

▶ Eddie very aptly demonstrates that it is possible to do bad things without being a bad person. This disparity should be discussed with the children. They need to see that Eddie is basically a good person who sometimes loses control of his behavior; i.e., he is not intentionally bad.

▶ It should be stressed that Eddie needs to get better at being in control. This, of course, is very different from saying or believing that he is bad and needs to become good. Such discussion can serve to reduce the guilt that some children with attention deficits sequester as they think of themselves as bad or immoral. The dialogue can have the added advantage of helping other students understand and tolerate the behaviors of a child with attention deficits.

---

## Helping Eddie Improve

**Understanding Oneself.** The benefits of having insight into oneself is a central concept throughout *All Kinds of Minds*.

**Points to Emphasize:**

▶ If Eddie is to improve, he must first understand that he has an attention deficit. This knowledge itself will help him strive to improve. (It's hard to fix a problem when you don't know what needs fixing.) Such insight demands more than a simple label (like ADHD).

▶ A child needs to have a clear understanding of his or her condition.

▶ Children also need to acquire a working vocabulary so that their problem can be discussed realistically.

**Taking Medicine.** The use of medication for treating attention deficits can be talked about, using Eddie's experience as the basis for discussion. Such discussion will be especially useful to students who are on medication or who may soon be taking drugs to help them with their attention problems. The following information can also be important to a student who has a friend, classmate, or family member who receives this form of treatment.

**Important Points:**

▶ The medicine does not make children smarter; it just helps them use their own abilities better.

▶ The medicine helps some kids concentrate better and it may make them less impulsive.

▶ The pills do not work well on all children with attention deficits. In some cases, pills don't help at all!

▶ There are different kinds of medicines that can be used. A doctor has to decide which one would be best to try.

▶ Taking medicine to help with attention is not something a kid should feel ashamed of.

▶ The medicine is never the whole answer. Kids need to keep working on their problems, too. And, even when they are taking medicine, kids also need to get help from grownups who know about attention deficits.

▶ Children don't take medicine forever. Sooner or later they shouldn't need it anymore.

Throughout the book, readers are introduced to different kinds of professionals who can help children. Eddie, for example, receives assistance from a pediatrician, from his own regular classroom teacher, and from a tutor. As they read *All Kinds of Minds*, children might maintain a list of the adults who are available when a child is having problems. Table 3 on page 51 of these guidelines shows such a list.

## MORE ABOUT ATTENTION AND ATTENTION DEFICITS

To review further different aspects of attention and attention deficits, one may want to review pages 233–240 in Chapter 8. There one can find a summary of the traits that accompany attention deficits, as well as a list of the ways in which children with attention deficits can help themselves.

### Core Messages in Chapter 2

1. The ability to concentrate well is very important for success in school.
2. Students have to concentrate on what they are learning and on how they are behaving.
3. When someone misbehaves, it does not mean he or she is bad. It means that the child needs to work hard on controlling his or her behavior
4. There are lots of things that can be done to help children with attention deficits.

# Chapter 3
# Sonya's Kind of Mind

**SONYA AS A PERSON**

Sonya is very typical of the many children who have difficulty acquiring reading skills in the early grades.

She experiences agonizing exasperation in her attempts to decode individual words for reading. Her problems processing language sounds represent what is currently thought to be a common cause of reading disorders in young children.

Sonya bears the added burden of the emotional turmoil she endures as a direct result of her learning disorder. Trying to read in front of the class causes Sonya to feel afraid and ashamed. Going for help from a learning disabilities teacher (Mr. Nasser) is painful, especially when classmates deride her. (Derek says Sonya is going to the "mental room.") When she is feeling especially defeated, Sonya declares that her teacher is mean, she hates school, and she doesn't care whether she ever learns to read or spell. Yet, Sonya is obviously a very sensitive and caring child.

Like Eddie and many of the other characters in *All Kinds of Minds*, Sonya can be viewed as a role model. Despite her problems, Sonya is able to use her talents (such as her good artistic and mechanical skills) to derive personal satisfaction and to enhance her relationships with others.

## DISCUSSING SONYA

### Interpreting Sounds—An Important Kind of Mind Work

Before discussing Sonya's plight, it can be useful to talk about the remarkable kind of mind work that enables human beings to interpret sounds.

---

**Points to Emphasize:**

▶ There is a big difference between *hearing* language sounds and *being able to interpret* them. This means that a person can hear well and still have trouble figuring out language sounds or recognizing them.

▶ For some children, recognizing language sounds and telling them apart from each other is very easy. For others, like Sonya, it is very hard.

▶ Our minds have to figure out lots of different kinds of information that comes in through our ears. For example, we must be able to tell whether a loud noise is thunder, whether that dog barking is *our* dog, and whether the teacher just said we will have a test tomorrow.

▶ Sounds that make up our language (the sounds we hear when someone is talking to us) are different from non-language sounds (like the sound of a car horn). They are also different from many of the sounds of other languages (like Chinese).

▶ Our minds have to learn to recognize all of the large number of sounds that make up our language—sounds like /ee/ and /th/ and /pl/.

▶ When you read or listen, you have less than a second to figure out the language sounds in most words, so this is one of the fastest kinds of mind work anyone does!

### Reading Disorders and Trouble with Language Sounds

There are some children who just cannot process language sounds accurately and fast enough. This makes it hard for them to learn to read.

**Trouble Recognizing the Sounds.** Children need to understand that, in order to learn how to read, a person has to recognize precisely every single language sound. He or she also needs to remember how different combinations of letters represent these language sounds (e.g., how *ight* might stand for the sound /ite/).

---

**Important Point:**

▶ If a child fails to recognize language sounds distinctly, she will find it extremely hard to match these sounds to letters. Consequently, she will have a great deal of trouble sounding out words. She will also find it difficult to spell.

---

The above explanation may be a little hard for some children to comprehend. (The same phenomenon is discussed in the text on pages 73–77.) The reading diagram on page 243 also may help with the discussion.

One may also want to use some analogies. For example, it is possible to cite as analogies for poor reception of language sounds some things like static in a radio or the trouble a person might have understanding somebody when there is a poor telephone connection.

**Trouble Blending the Sounds.** Children should be helped to understand that another part of decoding skill for reading involves the ability to *combine* sounds. This particular function is also problematic for Sonya.

> **Important Point:**
>
> ▶ In trying to decode a multisyllabic word, a child must figure out the sound of the first syllable or phoneme, and then the second syllable, and then the third syllable. Then he or she has to *reblend* the individual sounds into one word. If a child has trouble holding the first sound in memory while he is working on the third sound, he will be unable to put the whole word together again.

**Overcoming the Problem.** It is very important to be optimistic and upbeat in discussing the disorder of a child like Sonya. Children with this kind of disorder need to be encouraged to "hang in there" and not to give up.

> **Point to Emphasize:**
>
> ▶ Children like Sonya should be helped to understand that they *can* learn to read; however, they require much more practice or drill than other students. And, like Sonya, they may also need to get help from a learning disabilities specialist who knows how to assist children with this kind of problem.

**Issues Related to Siblings**

**An Issue Faced by Sonya.** Sonya also raises another major (and extremely common) concern; namely, what is it like for a child with a learning disorder to have a high-achieving sibling? This scenario is presented in Chapter 3 as Sonya must listen to her grandmother praising her brother Marco's outstanding reading skills (for which he has won a prize, no less!).

Sonya's painful and perhaps humiliating plight is worthy of discussion. The following questions can be raised:

**Questions for Children**

1. Can a child like Sonya feel jealousy or maybe even anger at her brother because he reads so well?

2. How do you think Sonya feels while her grandmother is praising Marco's reading ability?
3. How does Sonya act when this happens?
4. How *should* Sonya or anyone else act at such a time?
5. What could Sonya and Marco's grandmother have done differently?
6. Is it normal for brothers and sisters to compete with each other?
7. Would Sonya feel any different if Marco were older than she?

**How Sonya Handles Her Situation.** In the course of Chapter 3, we discover that Sonya compensates effectively for the imbalance in reading skills that exists between her brother and herself:

1. There are some things *she* actually teaches *him*. (She helps Marco with mathematics.)
2. As the chapter unfolds, we see that Sonya heroically "rescues" her brother and repairs his eyeglasses and his bicycle.

In other words, instead of trying to hurt her brother (as some children might do) out of jealousy and anger, Sonya actually finds ways to be helpful to him. This fortifies her role as an older sister and establishes a really solid relationship, despite the fact that Sonya does indeed feel jealous and angry about Marco's excellent reading skills.

---

**Important Points about Relationships with Siblings:**

▶ It is important to stress that it is quite natural for a child to feel very bad when there is something a sibling can do much better than she or he can. This is especially the case when that sibling is younger! It is normal for brothers and sisters to compete with each other and even to fight and argue sometimes. But through her compensatory actions, Sonya actually handles this situation extremely well.

▶ It would be useful to refer to Chapter 2 in the student's text ("Eddie's Kind of Mind") to point out that Eddie and Becky show some rivalry, too. They tend to make nasty comments to and about each other, yet it is very clear that they also have a close relationship and really care about each other.

*Important Points about Relationships with Siblings, continued*

▶ In both Chapters 2 and 3, the message is implicit: you can have very angry feelings toward a brother or sister and still feel real love and devotion toward that person.

## Sonya's Strengths

Sonya's chapter also vividly illustrates the point that a child may have very definite strengths and weaknesses. Sonya's reading disorder is clearly offset by her excellent spatial, fine motor, mechanical, and social skills. She is especially adept at visualizing and at understanding how things work. Thus, the chapter on Sonya brings forth a recurring theme in *All Kinds of Minds*: everyone has strengths and everyone has weaknesses. It would be useful at this point to review Sonya's strengths and her weaknesses.

**Important Point:**

▶ It would be relevant here to call students' attention to the fact that sometimes children keep thinking too much about their weaknesses and, therefore, fail to see the ways in which their minds are strong.

**Core Messages in Chapter 3**

1. To read well, children need to be good both at figuring out different language sounds and at putting the sounds together to make whole words.
2. Some kids have trouble with language sounds, so they have a reading disorder.
3. It is especially hard to have a problem with learning when you have a brother or sister who does very well in school.
4. If you don't give up, and if you accept help, your reading can improve a lot.

# Chapter 4
# Bill's Kind of Mind

**BILL AS A PERSON**

Bill is a confused and unhappy boy. He is highly competitive and craves success, yet his difficulties meeting the memory demands of school have created frustration for Bill in every subject area. He is much better at understanding than he is at remembering.

Behaving in school is sometimes a problem for Bill. He is aggressive and has trouble relating to other students, except when he is playing sports; his superior athletic skills are a "saving grace" for him. He is a great athlete; others always want to have him on their side during a game.

Another of Bill's interests is cars, and he enjoys sharing his expertise in this area with others. When he does so, he astounds his classmates with his vivid explanations of how engines work.

Bill expresses himself well (which suggests that he has strong language skills) and shows a quick wit, as exemplified in the joke he makes to his father at the end of the chapter.

Despite his multiple assets, Bill is clearly overwhelmed in school. He suffers profound feelings of inadequacy. He reacts to these feelings with intense anger and sometimes denial. (At one point, he tells his parents he just wants to be left alone.) At other times, Bill's low self-esteem is all too obvious, as he describes himself as "a loser, a total loser."

## DISCUSSING BILL

### A Memory Disorder

As we have just indicated, academic activities requiring the rigorous use of memory are often problematic for Bill. This problem occurs despite the fact that he has no difficulty processing language, comprehending explanations, and really grasping what is occurring in various mathematical processes. The disparity between understanding and remembering is evident when it is reported that Bill "understood how multiplication works, but he couldn't remember math facts like how much $8 \times 4$ is" (page 101).

Three kinds of memory problems are exemplified in Bill:

1. He has trouble retrieving very precise information (or a very precise skill such as letter formation) from memory when he needs it. It is noted that on his IQ test Bill has trouble remembering specific facts (page 100).
2. He has difficulty storing and defining sequences of information (i.e., material in which a specific serial order needs to be preserved). Thus, Bill has trouble remembering a list of numbers in the correct order (page 99).
3. He has problems holding several different ideas or processes in his memory at the same time. For example, it is very hard for Bill to remember spelling at the same time that he is trying to punctuate when he is writing a paragraph (page 101).

---

**Points to Emphasize:**

▶ Students who have problems with their memory can feel very bad about school. Even though they understand a lot of things, their trouble remembering makes them feel dumb.

▶ Memory plays a major role in school. Its varied applications are summarized in the chart on page 247. It is needed in every subject. Students may want to figure out which parts of a particular subject or skill require memory. Examples might be facts in math, spelling and punctuation rules in writing, and word appearances for reading.

*Points to Emphasize, continued*

▶ Memory is just like a closet or a dresser or a locker. You put facts or new skills into your memory so you can find them later on when you need them.

▶ It is important for students to think a lot about memory in school. For example, when they're trying to study for a test, they need to ask themselves: "Let's see—how am I going to remember this?"

Memory doesn't just work by itself; you need to "turn it on" by concentrating hard, repeating things you want to remember, testing yourself, and writing things down to help you remember them. These techniques are called "memory strategies." Such techniques are suggested to Bill (page 111) and are further reviewed on pages 251–252. Children should be encouraged to think up—and possibly list—other techniques.

**Activity for Children**

## Understanding Bill's Behavior

**Question for Children**

Bill's aggressive behavior raises many important issues, including his stealing. A fruitful discussion could result from asking children why they think Bill stole Becky's wallet.

**Points to Emphasize:**

▶ Sometimes kids misbehave without understanding why.

▶ Bill can't figure out *why* he took Becky's wallet (page 94).

▶ Bill acts tough because he does not want other people focusing on how poorly he does in school. Some children would rather be seen as behavior problems than as "dumbies." Bill's mother points out this possibility to him (page 96).

▶ Although Bill doesn't want her to, Mrs. Grillo *has* to tell Bill's mother about the stolen wallet. This is so his parents can know more about Bill's behavior and also so he can start to get help.

### Bill's Understanding of Bill

Another major issue in this chapter relates to Bill's insight into his own strengths and weaknesses. It is very clear that at the beginning of the chapter Bill has very little understanding of Bill!

---

**Important Points:**

▶ We witness a remarkable improvement in Bill's behavior once he acquires insight into his memory problems.

▶ Bill demonstrates the dangers of misunderstanding and the benefits of understanding clearly one's own strengths and weaknesses. He also exemplifies the fact that once you grasp the nature of your learning disorder, you have something very specific to work on and you don't feel globally "dumb."

---

### The Importance of Success

Bill's triumphs in sports dramatize how important it is for every child to be able to do something that is perceived by others as successful. In a sense, every child has to try to be good at something that most other children are not as good at. Sports can serve as one source of such gratification, but there can be many others as well.

**Activity for Children**

Children should be encouraged to list as many different examples of such "specialties" as they can. Specific hobbies, expertise in a particular area (such as Bill's knowledge of engines), musical or artistic skills, or experience with a particular kind of job all represent ways in which children can display competency and savor success even when they have a learning disorder.

### The Issue of Rewards and Punishments for Schoolwork

Bill's restriction from soccer yields several related ethical questions that children might enjoy pursuing:

**Questions for Children**

1. Is it fair for a student to be told that he can't play sports unless his schoolwork improves?

2. Should playing a sport or being able to do other things you really enjoy depend on the achievement of a particular grade in school (such as a B in reading), or should it depend mainly on behavior and getting work done?

3. Should a child who has a learning disorder ever be punished for his/her schoolwork? If so, when? (A response to this question might be that a child might be punished if she or he isn't even trying to improve.)

4. Should someone be given rewards for doing well or improving a lot in school?

Obviously, there are no absolutely correct or incorrect responses to these questions, but they are certainly worthy of deliberation and dialogue.

**Intelligence Testing**

Bill visits Dr. Silva, the school psychologist. It would helpful to discuss what a psychologist is and to emphasize that someone is not "dumb" or "crazy" if she or he goes to see one. Students should know that a psychologist like Dr. Silva is a person who knows how to test kids to find out about their strengths and weaknesses and to learn more about why they behave the way they do.

Since Dr. Silva gives Bill an IQ test, and since many young readers of this book may be given IQ tests, it would be appropriate to conduct some discussion about IQ tests and what it is they measure.

---

**Points to Emphasize:**

▶ A person's intelligence measures how well different kinds of mind work are done by him or her.

▶ There are many different ways to be intelligent. Some people may be intelligent at fixing things; others may be intelligent at music; and others may be intelligent at arithmetic. This makes sense since we know that there are all kinds of minds.

*Points to Emphasize, continued*

▶ Intelligence might include how well people remember things, how good they are at figuring out how the parts of objects fit together, and how accurately they understand language.

▶ IQ tests measure *some* of the ways to be intelligent. They don't measure all of the kinds of intelligence. There are many important strengths and weaknesses that are not tested by IQ tests. For example, IQ tests don't measure your imagination or your ability in art or music.

▶ IQ tests include many different kinds of games, puzzles, and questions that can help a psychologist find out about some of a child's strengths and weaknesses. Bill had to remember numbers and put together blocks (pages 98 and 99) during his IQ test.

▶ IQ testing is done on all kinds of students. The fact that a child is given an IQ test does not mean that people think she is stupid or weird.

▶ Getting tested can actually be fun and interesting— especially if someone explains to you all about how you did on different parts of the test. Remember, of course, no one has a perfect kind of mind on tests—or anywhere else.

## Achievement Testing

Bill's chapter also offers an opportunity to discuss achievement testing. Since most students have taken such tests and may wonder how they work, one can use Bill's experience to show how these assessments may be helpful in pinpointing exactly which academic skills are problematic. In Bill's case, the testing shows his trouble with math facts and with the recall needed for spelling and for writing mechanics.

## Helping Bill Improve

Bill's scenario also exemplifies the kinds of help that a student with a learning disorder can receive. He is working *both* on his learning (memory) disorder and on his academic problems in writing and mathematics.

---

**Points to Emphasize:**

▶ Bill is helped to understand as much as possible about his memory problems.

▶ Bill is taught some "strategies"—like whispering to himself (page 110)—to help with his memory problem.

▶ Sometimes Bill is allowed to do things—like use a calculator (page 113)—to work around his memory problem.

▶ When Bill understands himself *and* gets help *and* starts to improve his work, his behavior also improves. That shows that it is easier to behave when you're doing well, but it's also easier to do well when you behave well!

---

**Core Messages in Chapter 4**

1. Much of what students learn in school requires a memory that works well.
2. In school, it is possible to be good at understanding things and still have trouble remembering things.
3. There are many kinds of memory needed for school; therefore, there are many kinds of memory problems that kids can have.
4. Students can use strategies to make their memories work better.
5. Some children misbehave or act tough because they feel bad about how they're doing in school.

# Chapter 5
# Eve's Kind of Mind

## EVE AS A PERSON

Eve is a sensitive and compassionate young girl who earnestly cares about other people and wants to help them be happy. She remembers everyone's birthday and even goes to great lengths to protect a spider whose life is in danger (pages 121–122)! Eve is also a diligent worker, a conscientious student.

At the same time, Eve endures the effects of a significant language disorder. She has difficulty with the comprehension of language and with verbal communication. Consequently, success in school subjects and activities requiring language eludes Eve. Moreover, she is quite self-conscious about her disorder; she says very little—in part because language expression exacts so much effort and, in part, because she is ashamed of her speech.

It is clear that Eve feels very apprehensive in school. She senses that other students understand and speak much better than she does. She constantly fears public humiliation in the classroom.

## DISCUSSING EVE

### The Importance of Language

Eve's plight exemplifies dramatically the critical importance of language ability in school. Students should be led to think about the various uses of language processing and production and helped to see that a large proportion of learning demands good use of language. Such uses include understanding assignments, solving word problems, understanding what you are reading, answering questions in class, and writing well. Examples of language abilities are depicted in the diagram on page 254.

Students should sympathize with Eve and appreciate how hard school must be for someone who has trouble keeping pace with its language demands.

### Language Ability and Inability

There are many different components of language ability; therefore, there are different types of language disorders. Eve presents one example of language difficulty. Obviously, students need not acquire a grasp of the technicalities of language function. However, some insights are likely to be helpful to them; these are shown in the box below.

---

**Points to Emphasize:**

▶ Language has two big parts: *receptive* language, the understanding part of language, and *expressive* language, the communicating or talking or writing part of language. When you listen to the teacher explaining something, you need to use your receptive language skill. When you tell a story, you use your expressive language skill. (See again page 254.)

▶ Understanding and talking are activities that have to be done very quickly and accurately in school. You just don't have a lot of time to figure out what someone is saying, and also you don't have much time to figure out how to say things yourself!

▶ Some students have trouble understanding language. They have problems when someone talks in long sentences or says complicated things. Eve has that problem, so she is often confused during class. She even has trouble understanding assignments or what the teacher says she needs to do on a test (page 143). That makes her feel dumb.

*Points to Emphasize, continued*

▶ Some children have trouble using language correctly when they speak. Eve also has that problem. She talks very slowly and she has to stop and think a lot—even in the middle of sentences. It is hard for her to think of the right words to use. It is also difficult for Eve to explain things to people.

▶ Some children mostly have a hard time speaking, while others mainly have difficulty understanding. Unfortunately, Eve has both problems.

▶ Students who have trouble with speaking and/or understanding can also run into problems with reading and writing because you need good language ability to become strong in these skills.

▶ Some children have language problems that are not as severe as Eve's. They sound alright when they talk, and they can understand a lot, but they may have trouble with language that is pretty complicated (like the kind that's in a science or social studies book).

**Understanding Eve's Behavior**

It is very important for children to have a chance to talk about Eve's behavior as it relates to her language difficulties. It is evident that Eve is quite withdrawn when she is with other children. In discussing Eve's chapter, it would be helpful to have students try to discern the possible relationship between her withdrawal and her language problems. Students could be asked the following questions:

**Questions for Children**

1. Is it possible that Eve is very quiet and shy because she does not have confidence in her language abilities?
2. Do you think Eve is afraid her classmates might laugh at her because of the way she speaks? Do you think some of them have made fun of Eve in the past? How would you describe kids who would do this?
3. Does Eve think she sounds weird?

4. Is it possible that Eve just can't talk fast enough to keep up with the conversations of other children?
5. Do children sometimes get very quiet when they're feeling sad about something?

Children should be helped to see that *all* of these explanations may be correct in Eve's case.

### Eve's Handling of Her Problems

Out of desperation, Eve copes with her problem by running away.

---

**Points to Emphasize:**

▶ It is, of course, vitally important to help children recognize that running away from a problem is *not* a good solution. The correct response is to:
  1. try to understand your problem well;
  2. face your problem;
  3. get help with your problem;
  4. work on solving your problem.
▶ When you run away from problems, they just get worse and worse. This philosophy is, of course, one of the principal themes of *All Kinds of Minds*.

---

**Alternatives to Running Away.** Children should discuss the dangers of running away, the bad things that can happen to a child who runs away.

Children should also discuss alternatives to running away. This can be done by asking them the following questions:

Questions for
Children

1. What else could Eve have done when she was feeling so bad?
2. How could she have made better use of the adults in her life to get some help?
3. Could Eve's friends have helped her? How?
4. Would Eve have behaved differently if she understood more about her language disorder?

### The Importance of Understanding Yourself

Students should be helped to realize that Eve, like Bill, doesn't understand herself well enough. At the beginning of the chapter, it is clear that Eve has no idea why she is doing so poorly, why she is having trouble understanding, why it is so hard for her to speak properly and fluently with other children. When a child doesn't understand her learning disorder, she may think everything is wrong with her mind; so Eve believes she is dumb (page 141).

Bill felt almost the same way when he didn't understand his learning disorder—he believed he was a loser and was "born to fail" (page 96).

---

**Important Point:**

▶ It would be good to stress the importance of understanding exactly what your learning disorder is so you won't think your problem is much worse than it is.

---

### Eve's Depression

Eve is depressed. Largely because of her learning difficulties, she is very sad. She has low self-esteem. The terms *depression* and *self-esteem* should be defined and discussed with children.

---

**Points to Emphasize:**

▶ Someone is depressed when he or she feels very low a lot of the time.

▶ When you are depressed, you are extremely sad. When you're feeling that sad you worry a lot, and you may not feel like doing things you usually enjoy. (Eve, for instance, loses interest in playing the piano.)

▶ Your self-esteem is how good you feel about yourself.

▶ Your self-esteem is low if you think everyone else can do things better, looks better, or just plain is better than you are.

*Points to Emphasize, continued*

▶ Your self-esteem is high if you believe you are just as good as other kids and maybe even better at certain things.

Children need to be aware of these concepts, so that if and when they begin to feel depressed or suffer from low self-esteem, they can know that they need some help.

## HOW TO FEEL BETTER ABOUT YOURSELF

<table>
<tr><td>**Activity for Children**</td></tr>
</table>

There can be fruitful discussion of what a child should do when he is feeling low. Children can list steps that can be taken to increase self-esteem. These steps might include:

1. Talking to an adult (a relative, a teacher, a doctor, or a counselor) about your feelings.
2. Finding something you can do really well—like playing a sport, or playing a musical instrument, or drawing cartoons.
3. Looking ahead and trying to feel good about the future—dreaming about what you can do when you grow up and how much fun it will be.
4. Making sure you find people to be with who like you and admire you—like really good friends or some grownups.
5. Doing things to help other people feel good—like coaching or teaching younger kids. (Sonya did this with her brother.)

**Important Point:**

▶ Children need to understand that everyone needs to feel good about himself or herself. While we all have times when we feel low, there have to be enough times when we all feel good about who we are and what we are!

**Core Messages in Chapter 5**

1. Good language skills are needed for success in school.
2. Children with language disorders have a hard time either understanding or speaking or both.
3. When you feel bad about learning, you may feel like escaping or running away, but there are much better ways of handling these feelings.

# Chapter 6
# Derek's Kind of Mind

## DEREK AS A PERSON

Derek has a very inquisitive and retentive mind. He displays excellent academic skills, and he has a strong interest in science.

Regrettably, Derek has tremendous difficulty relating to his peers, whom he alienates with his comments and actions. He is boastful and sometimes physically aggressive. Because he has no friends, Derek spends much of his life in isolation. He has learned to entertain himself (e.g., he assembles a two-way radio), but he still craves companionship.

Derek is not at all an athlete; his interests are largely intellectual. He feels "different" and is quite self-conscious about his clumsiness as revealed in his reluctance to attend the class outing. Derek seems to have a good relationship with his parents, who are divorced. Relating effectively to adults and younger children is far easier for him than relating to kids his own age.

## DISCUSSING DEREK

### Having More Than One Learning Disorder

Derek has two kinds of learning disorders—a motor problem and a social skills problem.

> **Points to Emphasize:**
>
> ▶ It is important to point out that both motor problems and social skills problems don't always appear in the same children. It is possible to have good motor skills and poor social skills; it is similarly possible to have excellent social skills and poor motor skills.
>
> ▶ Different kinds of learning disorders can appear in any mixture in any child; so, for example, some kids may have trouble with attention and memory. Others have trouble with language and social skills. Still others may have difficulty with motor skills and memory.
>
> ▶ Some students have more than two kinds of learning disorders—and they are still smart in a lot of ways!
>
> ▶ There are so many different combinations of strengths and weaknesses of the mind; just about everybody is different from everybody else. This point is, of course, a recurring theme throughout *All Kinds of Minds*.

**Getting Along with Others—An Important Kind of Mind Work**

The concepts of social skills and of social skills problems merit discussion. Children need to understand that getting along well with people is a vital kind of mind work. The illustration on page 263 of the student's book delineates some major subcomponents of social ability. These aspects of social skill should be reviewed; and, when appropriate, students can be asked to give examples of the items in the boxes.

The following questions can be used to guide a discussion about social skills:

| Questions for Children |
| :--- |

1. How do other kids feel about a boy or girl who:
   a. Often talks funny, says weird things, and says things the wrong way?
   b. Never says things to make others feel good?
   c. Doesn't try to look right?

d. Doesn't share things and doesn't seem to trust other kids?

e. Boasts and brags a lot?

f. Acts too tough?

**Activity for Children**

2. What are the kinds of social mistakes that Derek makes? (Children could list Derek's errors; e.g., acting too tough, bragging, always trying to be first in line, putting down other kids, and not talking "right" with them.)

3. What's the difference between having some close friends and being popular? (Students need to be helped to see the difference between friendship and overall popularity. They need to realize that it is possible to have some close friends without being popular and that it is possible to be popular without having close friends!)

4. If someone has social skills problems:

a. How hard will it be for him or her to have a very close friend?

b. Will it be hard to be popular? (Children should understand that good social skills are needed for both popularity *and* friendship.)

5. Can a student be different from others and still have friends and be popular—if he or she wants to be? (This issue is important to pursue. Students should recognize that Derek *could* have social success even though he is not athletic and is interested in areas that not too many other kids like. Children need to see the difference between conformity and popularity.)

6. What are some of the excellent kinds of social skills that popular children and good friends have?

**Social Skills Problems As a Learning Disorder**

Social skills problems, like the other problems dealt with in *All Kinds of Minds*, must be understood well by the students who endure them. Then they can start working on improving their social skills just as Derek does.

Points to Emphasize:

▶ It is especially important to help children understand that people with social skills problems are really not to blame for their problems. They don't realize the mistakes they are making when they try to interact with others.

▶ Like Derek, most children with social skills problems feel lonely and want to improve.

▶ A social skills problem is like any other kind of learning disorder; and, therefore, it is inappropriate to make fun of or gang up on a child who is having trouble with social skills. Instead, everyone needs to help that boy or girl.

**Activity for Children**

At this point, it can be useful to have students make a list of all the things that Derek does to work on his social skills. (For example, he stops teasing and bragging.) They should also be encouraged to add their own ideas about what any child can do to have good social skills (share toys, praise others, etc.). Finally, children should talk about what kids can do to help a classmate who is having trouble with social skills (invite him to parties, sit with her at lunch or on the bus, etc.).

### Derek's Motor Problems

Derek, who has both fine and gross motor problems, is upset about his deficient motor skills. The material on pages 266–268 of Chapter 8 should help students appreciate the differences between fine and gross motor skills and facilitate discussion of these differences.

Derek's fine motor problems make it hard for him to do art work and various craft activities. He is very different from Sonya who is so good with her hands. Also, Derek's gross motor shortcomings (as opposed to Bill's talent in this domain) make him anxious and extremely self-conscious about his clumsiness. He performs so poorly at sports that he is forever being chosen last for teams. Physical education or after school athletic activities are often humiliating experiences for Derek.

**Points to Emphasize:**

▶ Clumsiness or trouble playing sports is *not* the fault of the child. (Sometimes peers will think that a poor athlete is just lazy or careless, that he *could* play well but that somehow he doesn't really try hard enough.)

▶ Some children's minds simply do not control their muscles very well. While they are playing a sport, it is too hard for them to get their muscles to do the right things, in the right order, fast enough.

▶ It is especially cruel for teammates to deride or embarrass a poor athlete because a child with gross motor problems can't help it if he or she plays poorly. (This point should be emphasized strongly!)

▶ Some children with motor problems may have trouble getting their minds to remember how to do things. The mind has to retain many different motor skills like how to tie shoelaces, ride a bicycle, or sign a name.

▶ Other kids have trouble concentrating on a sport, even though their muscles can be well controlled. (Eddie exemplifies this phenomenon.)

### Derek's Reactions to His Problems

Derek vividly reflects the agonies that may face children with motor disorders, even those who succeed in academic pursuits.

Derek is certainly in a state of panic as he faces the prospect of participating in the class trip to the lake. He is very much (and perhaps realistically) afraid that he will be humiliated when the children play kickball. Consequently, he tries to avoid going to the lake. He even belittles the excursion by saying that it "sounds boring to me—very, very boring" (page 163).

Students can profit from discussing Derek's reactions to his problems and the steps he takes to work on them. The following points and questions can be used to stimulate discussion:

**Questions for Children**

1. Derek handles his embarrassment about his problems in two ways: avoidance (staying away from what you're not good at)

and putting down (saying bad things about what you're not good at). How well do these things work for Derek?

2. Should someone like Derek be forced to go somewhere where he might be embarrassed in front of other children? (There really is no right or wrong answer to this question.)

3. Sometimes it is possible to compromise. Derek goes to the lake, but he takes pictures instead of playing ball. Is this a good solution?

4. Are there some ways Derek could improve in sports without getting embarrassed? (One example would be Derek's father working with him on weekends with nobody watching them. That way Derek has some privacy while he tries to get better.)

5. Should Derek work hard to get good at just one sport so he can feel better about his motor skills? (Derek actually does this when he works with his father on weekends.)

6. Does everybody need to play sports? Is being good at art or music or collecting things just as important as being good at sports? (During such a discussion, students should be aware of the importance of keeping one's body in shape. It should be pointed out that this can be accomplished by exercising or riding a bicycle or hiking, if a student is not involved in sports.)

---

**Important Point:**

▶ Complete avoidance of a difficult situation is never the best answer!

---

### Terriball and Its Significance

There are many relevant messages implicit in the game of Terriball, the lighthearted recreation invented by Eddie. Eddie tries to point out that sports are supposed to be fun. He implies that most people take games too seriously. Bill embodies this attitude.

Eddie suggests that if you worry too much about winning or think too hard about being the very best, the game is no longer a game because it stops being much fun. Eddie goes so far as to suggest that sometimes adults (such as coaches and parents) cause games to stop being games. All of this raises some critical issues regarding competitiveness, the need to win, and the importance of having real fun while you are playing.

Terriball is a highly creative and imaginative game. As such, it raises some questions:

1. Shouldn't children try to think up *new* games?
2. Aren't there benefits to brainstorming and attempting to devise one's own system of rules for play?
3. Is it sometimes stifling for youngsters just to keep on playing the same old games year after year?

In recent years, many professionals have voiced concern that children are engaging in fewer and fewer imaginative and imaginary games. They believe that this loss, combined with excessive television viewing and other passive intellectual activities, may ultimately take its toll on a child's creative development and impede the acquisition of potentially productive brainstorming skills (an ability Eddie thinks everyone needs to have, as shown on pages 226 and 227 of the student's book).

---

**Activity for Children**

**Points to Emphasize:**

▶ In discussion, it would be valuable to use the game of Terriball to emphasize to children the need to include in their play the use of their imaginations and creative abilities. As part of this discussion, one might wish to ask students to create a new sport.

▶ It is noteworthy that Eddie and Derek can enjoy playing Terriball without worrying about who is good at it and who isn't. In fact, Eddie makes a mockery of competitive sports by suggesting that Derek will be a champion if and only if he plays Terriball terribly! At the same time, Derek discovers that you can have a lot more fun with other children if you're not trying to compete with them or prove to them how great you are.

**Core Messages in Chapter 6**

1. Knowing how to get along with others is an important kind of mind work; for some kids it's easy, but others, like Derek, find it hard.
2. Children with motor problems can feel very bad about themselves; it is cruel to make fun of them.
3. Kids can improve their motor skills and their social skills if they get help.

# Chapter 7
# The Minds of All Kinds School

## LOOKING AHEAD

In Chapter 7, the children come together and in a fanciful manner begin to think about their own futures. This is apt to be a healthy activity, since many children with learning disorders have tremendous apprehension about what the future holds. (Bill has the notion, for example, that he was "born to fail.")

Through the use of Eddie's grownupulator, the children in *All Kinds of Minds* have an opportunity to ponder the ways in which their particular strengths and weaknesses may influence their future endeavors. The essential message in this chapter is that everyone has a wide range of productive pathways possible for later life. There are many different ways to make use of your strengths—both for a career *and* for having fun in life. This chapter is meant to be upbeat and optimistic.

### Exploring the Possible

| Activity for Children |
|---|

The adult conducting a discussion of Chapter 7 might ask children to think about each of the students in the book. The children should talk about all the different kinds of activities (both vocational and recreational) that each child might pursue to draw upon his or her strengths. Table 5 on page 52 of these guidelines shows some examples.

Each participant in the discussion might also speak of her or his own strengths and how they might someday be used in many different exciting and important ways.

**Points to Emphasize:**

▶ It is important to be thinking about how to make your strengths stronger.

▶ You don't have to give up on your weaknesses. You can be working on them, too. If you keep at it, your weaknesses will become less and less weak!

▶ Everybody has weaknesses—even when they look as if they're perfect and have nothing to worry about. Even Becky, who seems like such a super-perfect kid, has a problem—she sometimes wets her bed.

▶ There are many different ways to be successful and happy as a grownup. It might be easier to be a grownup than to be a kid because when you grow up you can spend most of your time doing what you're very good at!

▶ Even though *All Kinds of Minds* talks a lot about school and work, students need to realize that there are many other kinds of success for grownups, such as getting a whole lot of pleasure from one's family and friends, as well as from hobbies and interests.

▶ It's sometimes good to talk to your friends about your strengths and weaknesses. That way you and a friend can get to know each other better.

▶ In Chapter 7, the children have learned to stop feeling ashamed of their kinds of minds. They are talking quite openly about their abilities and their inabilities—and they are having fun doing it!

## THE MINDS OF ALL KINDS SCHOOL

In Chapter 7, the children also have an opportunity to discuss "educational policy," as they conjure up a school that would nurture all kinds of minds. The dream school is largely a creation of Eddie, but it meets with general acceptance and enthusiasm; each child finds a pivotal role to play based on her or his strengths.

Chapter 7 should help students think about and perhaps articulate the ways in which school is a problem or a potential problem for their kinds of minds. They should consider ways in which school might be a better experience for them if they could alter certain characteristics or procedures within the school.

Before they do this, children need to be helped to see the need of being broadly educated. They can't simply eliminate subjects or activities that their kinds of minds find difficult. There are, however, ways that schools can make life more comfortable for children with learning disorders. They can, for example, help them by:

1. Providing a tutor or learning disabilities teacher for students with reading disorders (page 242).
2. Shielding them from potential embarrassment. (For example, Mrs. Grillo lets Bill know in advance when she is going to call on him in class—page 112.)
3. Making every child feel important and special. (Every child can become an expert in some area—pages 221–222.)

**Activity for Children**

Thus, the Minds of All Kinds School can serve as a stimulus for children with learning disorders to explore—by means of discussing, writing, or drawing—what they might expect from an ideal school. Such an activity can be healthy for students, and it can even be informative to teachers, parents, and school administrators!

**CORE MESSAGES IN CHAPTER 7**

1. Everyone has a wide range of productive pathways possible for later life.
2. There are many ways to make use of your strengths both in a career and for fun.
3. It can feel good to be honest about your strengths and weaknesses.
4. It is really important for schools to be kind to every kind of mind.

# Chapter 8
# Time to Remind
# Your Mind

Chapter 8 is the nonfiction portion of *All Kinds of Minds*. There are many ways in which this chapter can be utilized for teaching purposes. As noted throughout these guidelines, the relevant sections and diagrams in Chapter 8 can be integrated into discussions of each child in the book and each type of learning disorder. Alternatively, Chapter 8 can be used for purposes of review after reading the entire book.

The various lists and diagrams in Chapter 8 may also find application over an extended period of time. A child who is receiving help can be referred back to these pages to talk about the specific subcomponents of his or her problem and the extent to which each of these is improving. For example, a student getting help with his social skills may return periodically to the diagram on social abilities (page 263) and think about his progress in each of the indicated aspects.

## LOOKING BACK AT *ALL KINDS OF MINDS*

It can be instructive to devote time to comparing the children in the book to each other with respect to a variety of issues. Tables 1–6 on pages 50–53 of these guidelines represent an attempt to illustrate these comparisons and make other important points. An adult can refer to these tables in discussions that compare the children in *All Kinds of Minds*.

## SOME ADDITIONAL ISSUES FOR DISCUSSION

There exists a nearly endless array of issues that can emanate from *All Kinds of Minds*. During a lively discussion, students are likely to raise some of these issues on their own. The following are some general topics that might be covered in reviewing and overviewing the text:

<table>
<tr><td>

**Questions for Children**

</td><td>

**1. Dealing with Embarrassment or Shame.** This is a theme that pervades most of the chapters; thus, it is a good overall issue to discuss with students. They might be asked:

</td></tr>
</table>

a.  What are you supposed to do if you feel ashamed about getting help for your learning disorder?

Possible responses:
- Talk to your teacher about it.
- Ask your teacher to explain to your class that you have a learning disorder but you're not "dumb" or "stupid."
- Don't worry about it because the other kids will get used to it and not say anything about it.

b.  Should you be afraid the other students will find out you have a learning disorder?

Possible responses:
- Yes, it is something to worry about.
- No, you shouldn't worry because so many kids need help with something in school.
- No, because you can get other kids to like you because of your strengths.

c.  Whom should you tell about your learning disorder? Your friends? Your brother or sister? Your other relatives?

Possible responses:
- You tell whomever you really trust.
- You tell a few people but not everyone you know.
- You tell all the people you are with a lot; once they understand, they'll realize that having a learning disorder is "no big deal." It doesn't mean you're dumb or anything like that.

d. What should you do if a kid makes fun of you because you have a learning disorder?

Possible responses:
• Ignore him or her.
• Have a talk alone with that student to explain your learning disorder.
• Ask your teacher or some other adult to have a talk with the kid who is making fun of you.

Questions for Children

2. **Being Treated Differently.** The issue of the fairness of "special treatment" for a child with a learning disorder is likely to arise in many classrooms. Some relevant questions emerge:

a. Should a child (like Eddie) with attention deficits be allowed to get up and walk around more than other students?

Possible responses:
• Yes, it helps him concentrate.
• Yes, as long as he doesn't bother anyone else.
• Yes, as long as he doesn't walk around just to have fun.

b. Should someone (like Bill) with a writing problem be allowed to write less than the other kids?

Possible responses:
• His writing will never get better unless he writes a whole lot.
• He should be allowed to write a little less than other kids because writing takes him such a long time.
• He should be allowed to write less in class if he is also practicing his writing at home—so someday he won't need to write less.

c. Should a student (like Sonya) with a reading problem be told that she doesn't have to read out loud in front of the other students?

Possible responses:
• Yes, so she won't have to be embarrassed.
• Yes, as long as someone is helping her to read better so that eventually she will be able to read out loud in front of people.

These accommodations are often called "bypass strategies." They certainly highlight the issue of fair and equal treatment. It might be good to point out that *every student* (even those without obvious learning disorders) should feel good to know that teachers can be flexible in what they expect.

**3. Assuming Responsibility.** Children with learning disorders must realize that they cannot "cop out" or avoid responsibility on the basis of their learning problems.

There can be some discussion of the things that students with learning disorders are responsible for:

a. Continuing to work hard.
b. Trying to use strengths.
c. Agreeing to accept help.
d. Working on improving their weaknesses at least a little bit each day.
e. Talking to an adult when they are feeling discouraged or unhappy about their trouble.

**4. The Role of Parents.** The role of parents is a valid issue for review. In each chapter of *All Kinds of Minds*, parents turn out to be highly sympathetic and supportive.

It should be acknowledged that not all parents have the time or ability to help their kids learn, but all parents can talk to their children about their problems and try to get the right kind of help for them.

Most of all, students need to be helping themselves. (They can do this, for example, by practicing in their weak skills areas, by developing good learning strategies, and by working hard in school.)

There can be fruitful discussion about what parents should and should not do to help children with learning disorders. Questions might include:

**Questions for Children**

a. How should a parent help with homework?

Possible responses:
• Be around when a kid needs some help with a homework assignment.

- Help a student get organized.
- Help a student get started.
- Check the work when it's completed.
- Parents should not do the work for the child.

b. Is it okay for a parent to keep reminding ("hassling") a kid about homework?

Possible responses:
- It's good for parents to keep reminding a kid about work that needs to be done.
- Parents should not overdo it by reminding a kid too often.
- Parents shouldn't sound angry when they do their reminding.

c. What should a parent do when a child is not working hard in school?

Possible responses:
- Find out what kind of learning disorder is making it difficult for a kid to work harder.
- Give the student rewards for working hard.
- Use some form of punishment.

d. What should a parent say or do when a kid talks about her problems in school?

Possible responses:
- The parent should try to understand the child's learning disorder.
- A parent should encourage a kid not to get discouraged.
- Parents should show that they are sympathetic.
- They should give the child some advice about how to do better.
- Parents might be able to arrange for an evaluation (testing) to find out more about a child's strengths and weaknesses and how the child can do better in school.

e. How can parents be most helpful?

Possible responses:
- Assist with homework.
- Help study for a test.
- Talk to the child's teacher about the learning disorder.
- Keep giving the student a chance to do things that she is good at (like music or sports or fixing things) in order to feel better about herself.

After students discuss the role of parents, they might think about the following question: What should a kid say or do if he thinks he is disappointing his parents because of his schoolwork?

Possible responses:
- Find other ways to impress them.
- Have a good long talk with his parents so they can understand how he feels about being "disappointing."
- Let them know he's really working on his problem.

**5. The Role of Pets.** On a lighter note, children may want to have some discussion about the dogs who play such a supportive role in *All Kinds of Minds*. While students are discussing the pets, they should realize that there are substantial differences between the kinds of minds these dogs possess. (See Table 6 on page 53 of these guidelines.) The dogs in the children's book face some of the same issues that confront their human companions.

We also learn a critical lesson when the dogs ultimately discover and admire the smelling and digging talents of Hot Fudge, until then the least respected member of the pack. The implicit message is that we all have within us some very real strengths that are waiting to be discovered by ourselves and others!

## THEMES TO DISCUSS

Some recurring themes emerge as students read or listen to the text of *All Kinds of Minds*. These themes should be reviewed and discussed with students as a way of summarizing the book's most important ideas.

### Recurrent Themes in *All Kinds of Minds*

1. There are many different kinds of minds that are good at different kinds of mind work.
2. A child has a learning disorder when his or her kind of mind has trouble with an important kind of mind work for school.
3. Often a learning disorder can make a student feel sad or act badly.
4. It is very important for a student with a learning disorder to understand all about the disorder and about his or her strengths, as well.
5. When someone has a learning disorder, he or she can still be very smart and do some kinds of mind work well and easily.
6. It is important to get over feeling too ashamed or scared about a learning disorder.
7. Children with learning disorders can get good help from adults.
8. Kids with learning disorders can do a lot to help themselves, too.
9. Students with learning disorders can and do become successful when they grow up—especially if they know how to use their strengths.
10. When a child has problems with behavior, understanding the reasons for the poor behavior will help the child improve it.
11. No one with a learning disorder should ever give up!

## ALL KINDS OF LIVES

Page 275 of *All Kinds of Minds* presents a somewhat philosophical statement intended to capture an overriding sense of optimism that infuses the book.

At this point, it can be helpful for students to try to think about some of the important kinds of jobs that need to be done in the adult world so we can all survive and lead good lives. Obviously, the list of such jobs could be endless, but students can have fun listing *some*. As alternatives to making a list, students can draw pictures or create a collage. As they do this, students should be helped to think about the kinds of minds that can accomplish these extraordinarily varied missions.

By engaging in this activity, students should gain a strong sense that we desperately need all kinds of minds to accomplish all the different kinds of mind work required in the adult world. Therefore, they should realize that each child must feel good about his or her kind of mind and the kinds of contributions it can make some day—maybe even starting right now!

> **Activities for Children**

**Table 1: Examples of Strengths and Weaknesses**

| CHILD | STRENGTHS | WEAKNESSES |
|-------|-----------|------------|
| Eddie | Imagination; Kindness; Social Skills; Reading | Attention; Control of Impulses; Writing |
| Sonya | Math; Fixing Things; Art; Decorating | Figuring out Sounds; Reading; Spelling |
| Bill | Sports; Cars/ Engines; Understanding Ideas | Memory; Math; Writing |
| Eve | Kindness; Art; Music; Handwriting; Memory | Reading; Language Use/ Understanding |
| Derek | Academic Work; Languages; Science; Memory | Social Skills; Motor Skills; Playing Sports |

**Table 2: How the Children Handle Their Problems**

| CHILD | HOW HE/SHE HANDLES THE PROBLEMS |
|-------|----------------------------------|
| Eddie | Possibly by clowning |
| Sonya | By putting down school |
| Bill | By acting tough; By putting down school |
| Eve | By running away |
| Derek | By trying to avoid; By putting down activities and people |

**Table 3: The Kinds of Adults Who Help the Children**

| CHILD | ADULT(S) | ROLES |
|---|---|---|
| Eddie | Pediatrician (Dr. Bronson) | Helps figure out learning and attentional problems; Checks health; Uses medicine; Gives advice |
| Eddie | Tutor | Assists with schoolwork and attention strategies |
| Sonya | Learning Disabilities Teacher (Mr. Nasser) | Works on building academic skills; Teaches how to do better in schoolwork |
| Bill | Psychologist (Dr. Silva) | Helps figure out learning/attentional/behavior problems; Gives advice on how to improve |
| Bill | Learning Disabilities Teacher (Ms. Laski) | Works on building academic skills; Teaches how to do better schoolwork; Helps enhance memory ability |
| Eve | Speech and Language Therapist (Ms. Goldberg) | Helps improve understanding and use of language |
| Derek | Social Worker (Mr. Thompson) | Helps with personal problems, like trouble with social skills |
| Everyone | Classroom Teacher (Mrs. Grillo) | Helps children do better in the classroom and not be embarrassed about their problems |
| Everyone | Parents | Listen; Advise; Care; Love |

**Table 4: Some Things That Help Children in *All Kinds of Minds* with Their Learning Disorders**

Being tested to find out all about the learning disorder and also about strengths

Receiving help to get a good understanding of the learning disorder

Getting advice about handling problems (like being made fun of) that are caused by the learning disorder

Doing things (like learning memory strategies) to strengthen weaknesses

Receiving tutoring to improve academic skills and work habits

Taking medicine to strengthen attention

Having some special arrangements (like using a calculator for math) in the classroom

Using strengths (like trying to learn visually) a lot

Getting help from a specialist (such as a speech and language therapist)

Never giving up!

**Table 5: Examples of How the Children Might Use Their Strengths When They Grow Up**

| CHILD | STRENGTH | USE FOR FUN | USE FOR WORK |
|-------|----------|-------------|--------------|
| Eddie | Imagination | Telling stories | Inventing things |
| Sonya | Fine motor skill | Making models | Repairing things |
| Bill | Gross motor skill | Playing sports for fun | Being a coach |
| Eve | Caring about people | Reading biographies | Counseling young people |
| Derek | Science ability | Collecting rocks | Being a scientist |

**Table 6: The Dogs and Their Kinds of Minds**

| DOG | OWNER(S) | KIND OF MIND |
|-----|----------|--------------|
| Hot Fudge | Eddie and Becky | Timid; Gets picked on; Possesses excellent digging skills |
| Chewsy | Sonya and Marco | Slow runner; Possesses excellent chewing skills |
| Napper | Bill | Very sensitive; Possesses outstanding sleeping abilities |
| Barktalk | Eve | Possesses strong dog language and barking skills |
| Superstar | Derek | Possesses good gross motor skills; Great at all dog sports |

N.B., In the interest of fairness, it is important to acknowledge the role of Bill's feline, Cool Cat, who shows tremendous strengths in her soothing skills when Bill is in distress!